# Rolling Along

## *The Story of Taylor and His Wheelchair*

McGraw Hill SRA

*Columbus, OH*

To my loving parents, Jack and Joyce Riggio, for the love and guidance they give to me daily. I love you.

*Special Thanks*

To Taylor and Tyler and their parents, Twana and Jeffery, for graciously allowing me to share a wonderful piece of their life with others.
To Kathryn Danian, physical therapist, for her patience during the countless moments I interfered with Taylor's therapy sessions; and to Camille, Michael, Alex, and Grant for their participation in the book.
To my husband, Bobby, for encouraging me to reach my personal goals, and to my three beautiful children, Dominic, Grant and Gianna.

*—J.R.H.*

First published in the United States under the title ROLLING ALONG: The Story of Taylor and His Wheelchair by Jamse Riggio Heelan, Rehabilitation Institute of Chicago, illustrated by Nicola Simmonds.

Published by arrangement with Peachtree Publishers.

**SRAonline.com**

McGraw Hill SRA



Printed in the U.S.A.

Send all inquiries to:
SRA/McGraw-Hill
4400 Easton Commons
Columbus, OH 43219

ISBN 978-0-07-612520-3
MHID 0-07-612520-3

12 BRP 23

The McGraw-Hill Companies

# Rolling Along

*The Story of Taylor and His Wheelchair*

Jamee Riggio Heelan, OTR/L
Rehabilitation Institute of Chicago

Illustrations by Nicola Simmonds

McGraw Hill SRA

Columbus, OH

Hi. My name is Taylor. I have a twin brother, Tyler, who looks a lot like me. He's also my best friend.

We both like to eat chocolate ice cream, wrestle with each other, and watch the Chicago Bulls play basketball. We both like to read about dinosaurs.

But unlike Tyler, I was born with cerebral palsy. That's what my doctor calls my condition. It causes my brain (the cerebral part) to tell my muscles to jump (the palsy part) instead of moving smoothly.

Tyler can run, jump, and skip, but because I have cerebral palsy, it's hard for me to walk.

For a long time I've used braces on my legs and a walker to help me move. Every week I visit a physical therapist named Kathryn. She stretches my muscles and then helps me practice balancing and working my muscles.

I have lots of friends in therapy. Some of them use braces or wheelchairs because like me, they have never been able to get around without special equipment. Others are in therapy because they were in accidents. Some can't move their arms or legs at all. We're all in therapy to get stronger.

Kathryn taught me how to use
my walker, which helped me
walk on my own two feet.
I could go short distances by myself
with it, but I moved very slowly
and got tired easily.

When I went to and from therapy,
my mom had to carry me.
Sometimes I got frustrated
because I had to depend on
other people so much.

When Kathryn let me try using a wheelchair in therapy, I was so excited. Tyler pushed me around in it because it was hard for me to get it to move on my own.

At first I thought I would roll in the wheelchair as fast as I wanted and that moving around would be easy. But I had to practice a lot. I had to make my arms strong and learn how to roll the wheelchair back and forth, how to turn, and how to use the brakes to stop the wheelchair from rolling.

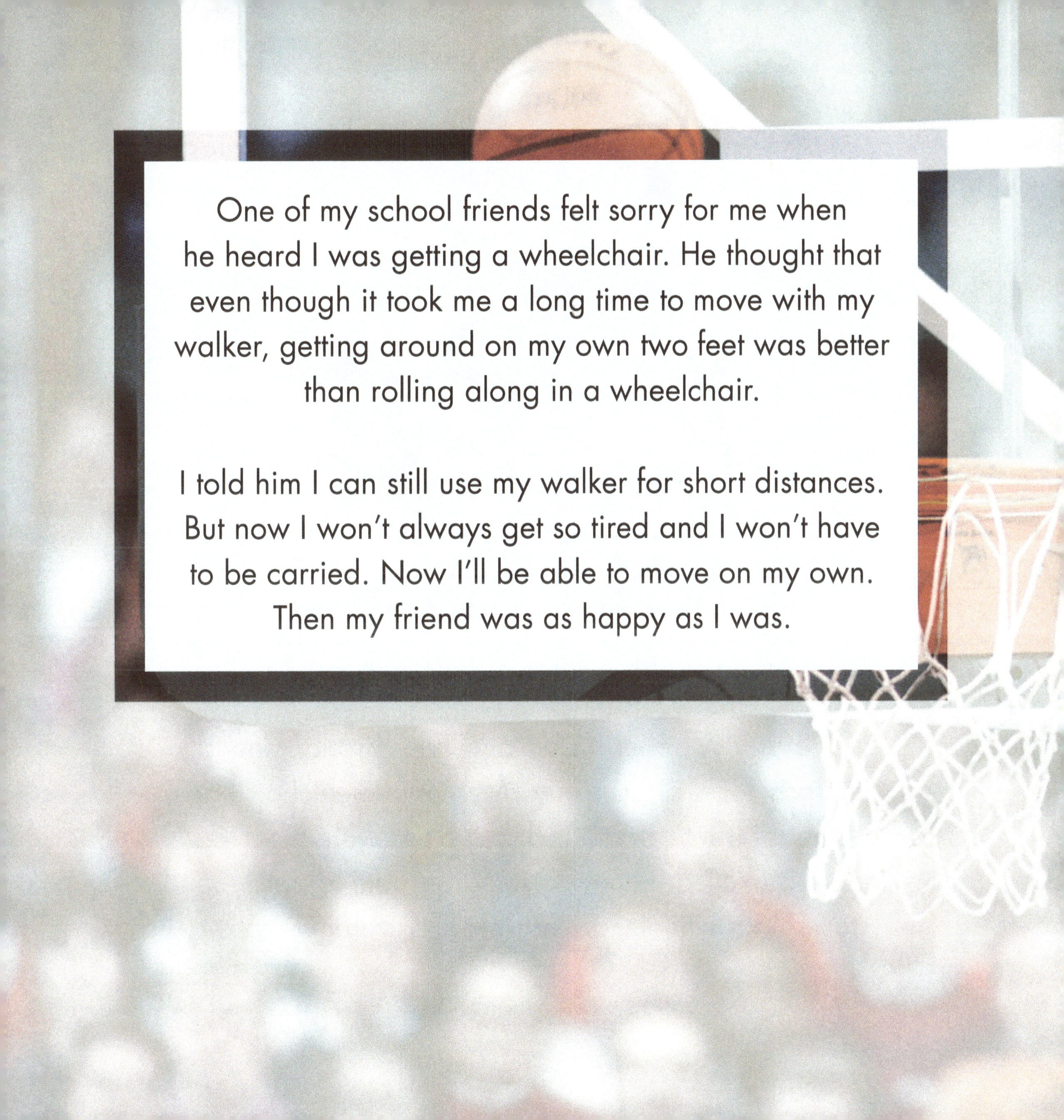

One of my school friends felt sorry for me when he heard I was getting a wheelchair. He thought that even though it took me a long time to move with my walker, getting around on my own two feet was better than rolling along in a wheelchair.

I told him I can still use my walker for short distances. But now I won't always get so tired and I won't have to be carried. Now I'll be able to move on my own. Then my friend was as happy as I was.

One day, Mom and Dad and Tyler brought me to therapy for a big surprise. My new wheelchair had come in! It was bright red and blue, with thick tires. I was so excited. I knew I would be able to get around faster in a wheelchair than I could with my walker.

Now I can turn to the right and left and I'm even learning how to "pop a wheelie," which means making the wheelchair's front wheels pop up in the air. That way I can get over bumps or big cracks in the sidewalk.

Tyler helps me practice wheelies by pulling back on my wheelchair handles and stepping on the lower bar. This lifts up the front of the chair a little. Then I balance myself in the chair and try to get over the bump. When I'm a little bigger and stronger I'll be able to pop a wheelie all by myself.

Now I need to pay attention to things that people who aren't in wheelchairs don't have to worry about. If a building has stairs at the front entrance and no ramp, I can't roll myself up to the door. If it's heavy front doors don't open with a button, I can't go inside. If the building has stairs or an escalator inside and no elevator, I can't get to the other floors.

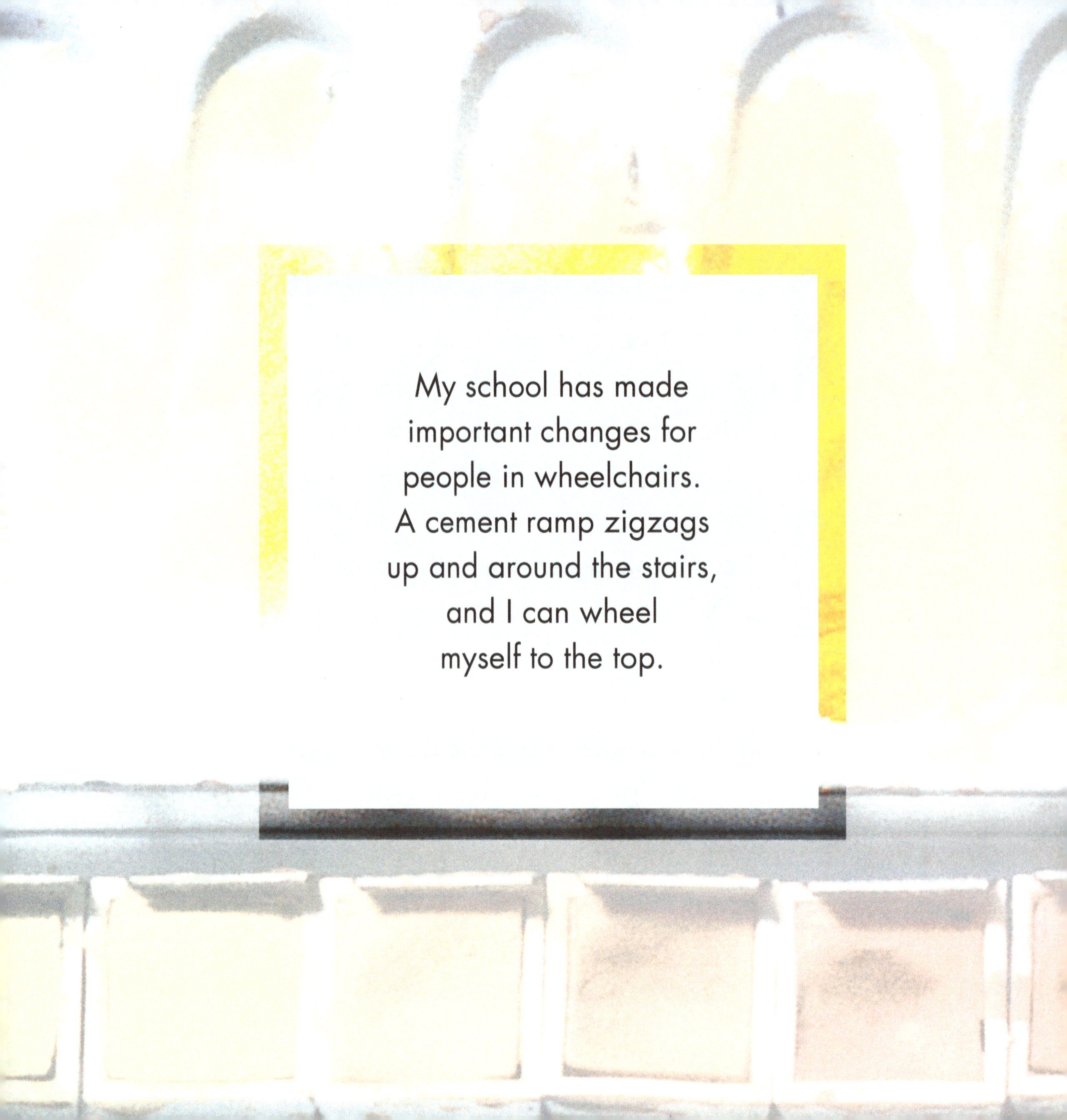

My school has made important changes for people in wheelchairs. A cement ramp zigzags up and around the stairs, and I can wheel myself to the top.

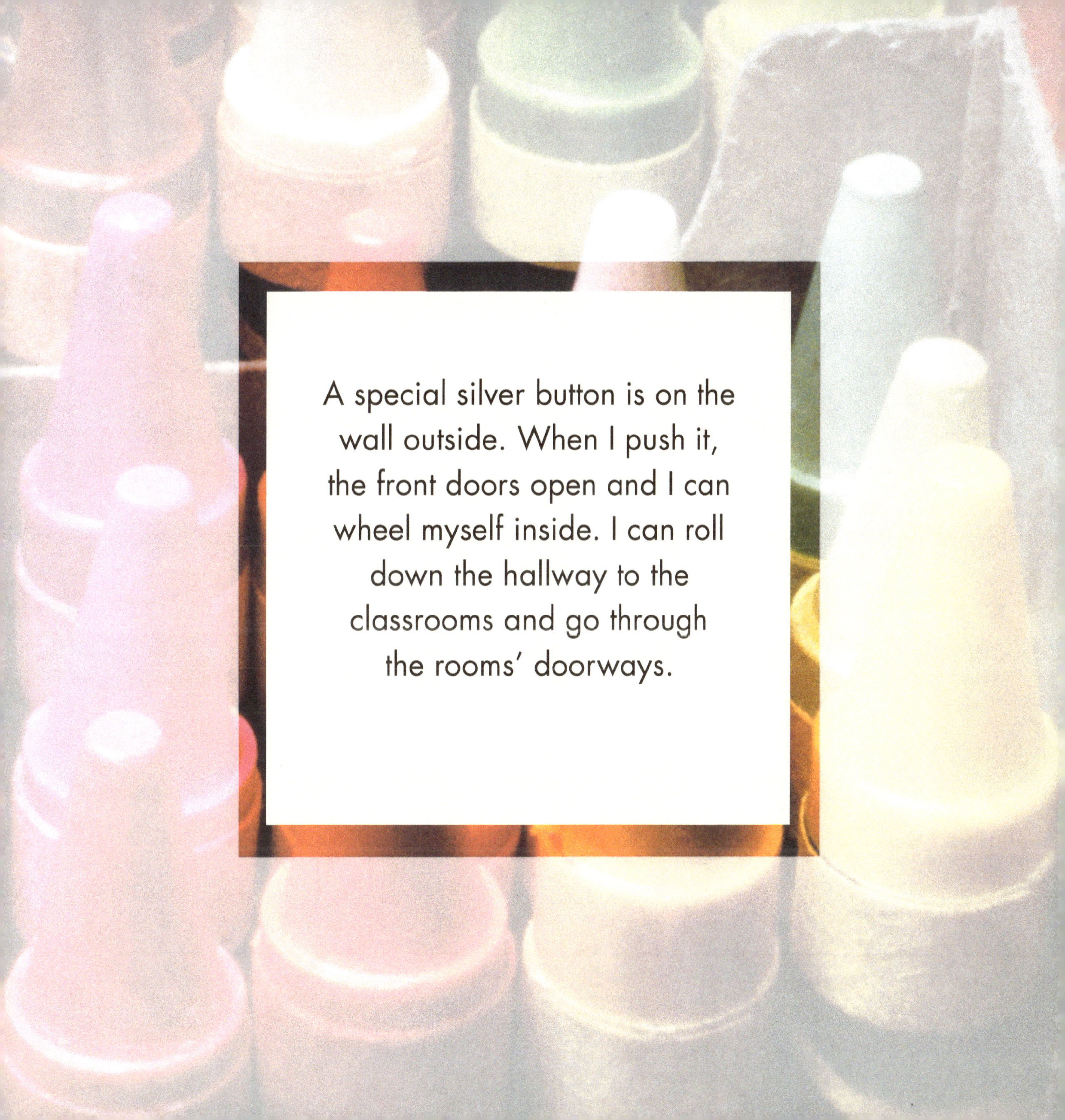

A special silver button is on the wall outside. When I push it, the front doors open and I can wheel myself inside. I can roll down the hallway to the classrooms and go through the rooms' doorways.

I can get a drink of water all by myself from the water fountain. It's just the right height for people in wheelchairs. I can wash my hands at the lower sink and I can even get in the large bathroom stall. It has a wide door that opens out so my wheelchair and I can fit inside.

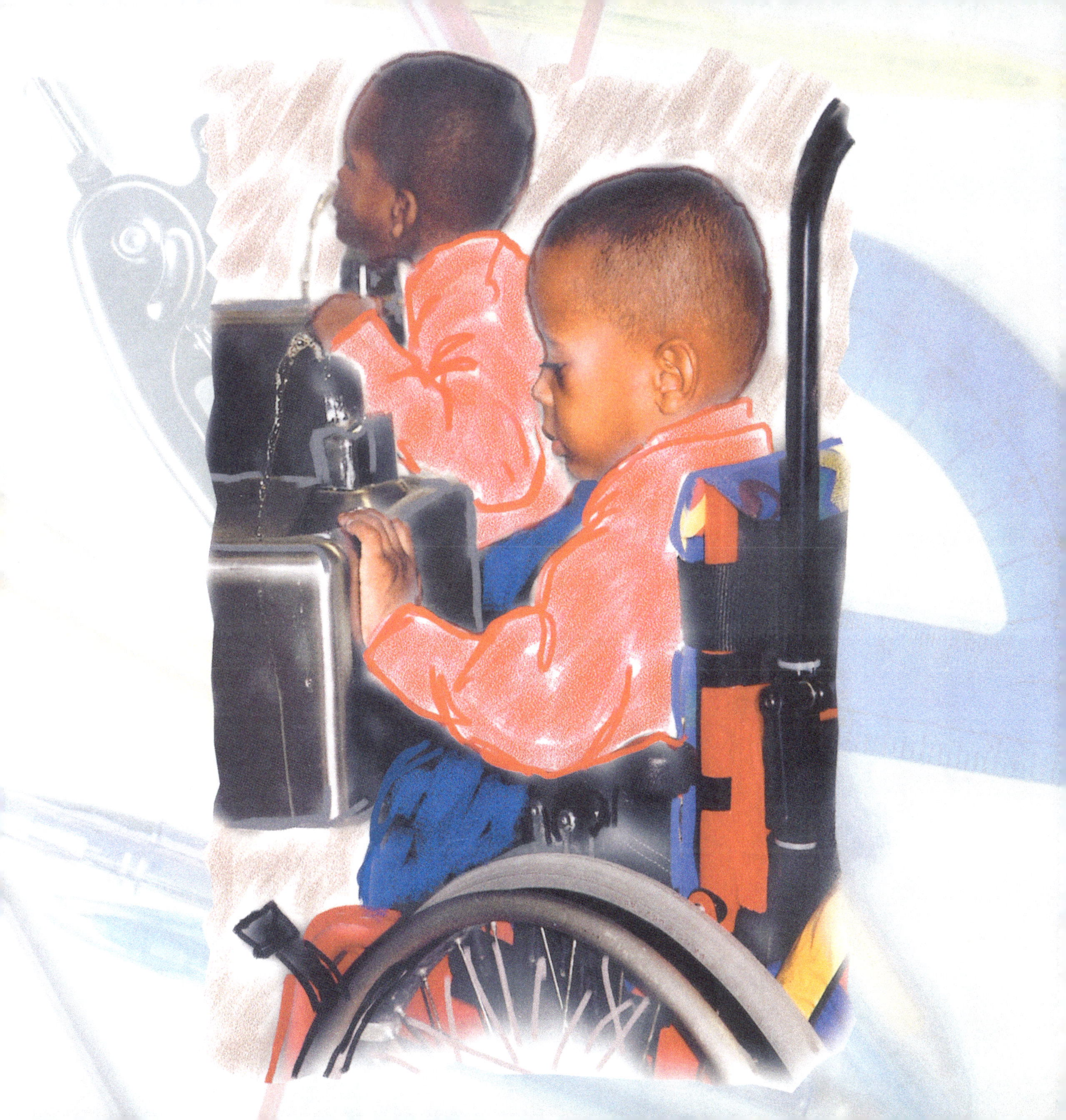

When I get home from school I lock my brakes and give my wheelchair a rest. Tyler helps me do my leg stretches. When we're finished, Mom lets us go outside to play.

My wheelchair lets me do a lot, like play all kinds of different sports with Tyler. Our favorite is basketball. Tyler runs on his two feet and does a layup. I push and steer my wheelchair with one hand and dribble the ball with my other hand. I roll as quickly as I can to the basket in my wheelchair and use both hands to shoot. It's hard, but I'm getting better and better. Sometimes I score as many points as Tyler.

My wheelchair helps me go more places on my own and do more of the things I want to do. Now nothing can stop me.